JESUS, HAVE YOU GOT A LIGHT?

Robert Kirkwood

Illustrated by Edward McLachlan

LONGMAN

Dedicated to:
C Edwards, Keith Seller,
Reginald Simpson, Ray Scholl

Acknowledgements

We are grateful to the following for permission to reproduce copyright material:

The Bible Society for Bible text from the Good News Bible © American Bible Society, New York, 1966, 1971 and 4th edition 1976, published by The Bible Societies/HarperCollins; Faber and Faber Ltd for the poems 'Warty Bliggens the Toad' by Don Marquis from *Archy and Mehitabel.*

We are grateful to the following for permission to reproduce copyright photographs:

Andes Press Agency/Carlos Reyes p. 34; Barnaby's Picture Library, p. 19 (Nick Hedges), p. 44 (David Simson); John Cleare/Mountain Camera, p. 32 bottom; Lucien Freud/James Kirkman Ltd p. 17 (both); Mansell Collection, p. 14 (all); Rex Features, p. 35 top; The Samaritans, p. 36; Shelter/Stuart McPherson, p. 35 bottom; Geoff Ward, pp. 9, 10, 11, 25, 35 (middle), 44.

Published by
Longman Group UK Limited
Longman House, Burnt Mill, Harlow,
Essex, CM20 2JE, England
and Associated Companies throughout the world.

First published 1992

ISBN 0 582 04582 7

Set in 14/16 point Gill Sans
Produced by Longman Singapore Publishers (Pte) Ltd
Printed in Singapore

CONTENTS

Being in the dark

Being lost and trying to find your way in the dark is not everybody's idea of fun.

The reasons are obvious. The darkness stops us from **seeing where we are going**. It is also scary because it prevents us from **seeing things as they really are.**

When however the lights come on, things are very different.

We can now **see the way ahead** and things around us no longer scare the living daylights out of us.

Questions and tasks

1 Why do you think that so many people are afraid of being alone in the dark? Try to think of many different reasons.

2 Imagine your Mum and Dad are out for the night and you are sitting alone at home watching the television. Suddenly you feel the need to go to the toilet. Unfortunately, the toilet is in a *dark* corridor with no light to switch on. Would you go or would you sit tight and cross your legs? Give reasons for your answer.

3 Draw a picture or write a poem to show the sorts of thoughts and feelings that go on inside you when you are alone in the DARK.

THE TEACHINGS OF CHRISTIANITY

The teachings of Christianity say that 'being lost' and 'trying to find your way in the dark' is very much like life itself.

These teachings say that life itself is a journey in which we are all trying to FIND THE RIGHT WAY to live in this world.

These teachings also say that we all have problems finding this way because we are 'lost' and 'walking in darkness'.

Now the ‘darkness’ that Christianity talks about is not the sort that happens when light-bulbs explode. This ‘darkness’ is the darkness of not understanding. In other words, BEING IN THE ‘DARK’ about what life is all about.

It is this ‘darkness’, say these teachings, which stops us from **finding the right way to live in this world**.

This ‘darkness’ also makes our journey through life scary because it stops us from **seeing things clearly**.

The teachings of Christianity also talk about a LIGHT which can lighten up our 'darkness'.

This 'light', according to these teachings, is **Jesus Christ — the light of the world.** He is called 'the light' because it is said that his life and his teachings can help us SEE THE RIGHT WAY TO LIVE IN THIS WORLD and can also make life less scary by showing us the things of life *as they really are*.

This book will be looking at some of the things which Christians say they can 'see' in 'the light' of the life and teachings of Jesus Christ. The titles of the following chapters are therefore all about **seeing**.

Tasks

Seeing is deceiving

1 People often say 'I will only believe what I see'. They say this because they are convinced that their eyes show them things *as they really are*. Our eyes, however, do not always tell us the truth. Sometimes they play tricks on us; they make us see things which are not there at all. Look at the following examples.

THE PHANTOM SAUSAGE

Bring your index fingers together about 45 centimetres in front of you. If you focus your eyes on the tips of your fingers, the fingers appear normal. Focus your eyes on a distant wall, and something very unusual happens: a short two-ended finger, looking like a small sausage, appears between your fingertips. Separate your fingers slightly and this miniature hot dog remains hanging in the air.

SEE THROUGH YOUR HAND

Roll a sheet of paper into a tube about 25 millimetres in diameter. Look through this tube with your left eye. At the same time look with your right eye at your hand, held beside the tube (see photograph). Although you know it cannot be true, a hole appears in the middle of your hand through which you can see objects beyond it.

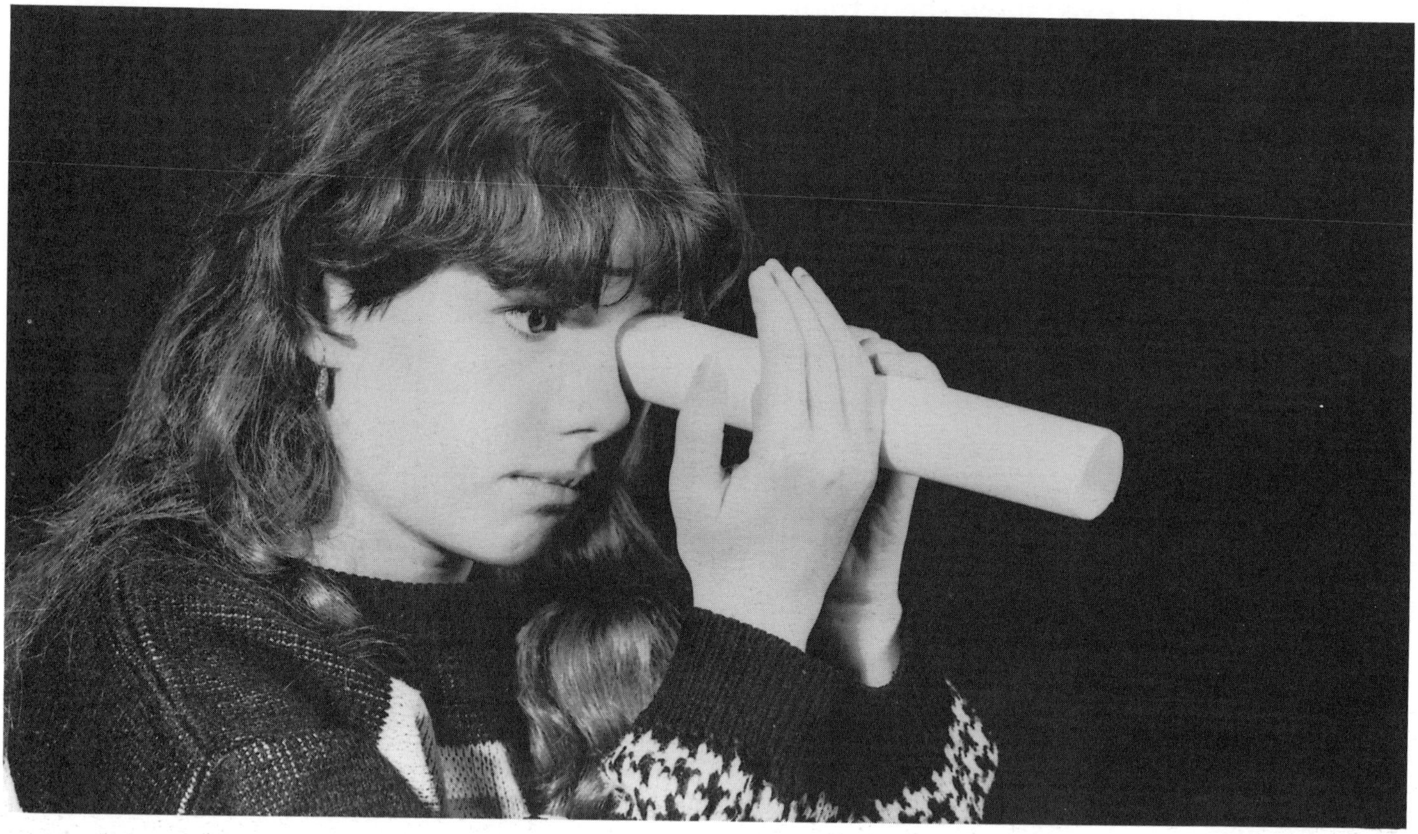

SEE A GHOST

Hold this page under a strong light and stare at the skeleton head for about 30 seconds. Then look away toward a dimly lit blank wall. Within seconds you will see a white face with black eyes, nose and teeth outlined in black projected against the wall. For the next few minutes you will see this ghost everywhere, even when you close your eyes.

2 Our eyes do not always trick us by making us see things which are not there. Sometimes they simply *distort what is there*. Look at the following examples and explain what illusions our eyes are creating.

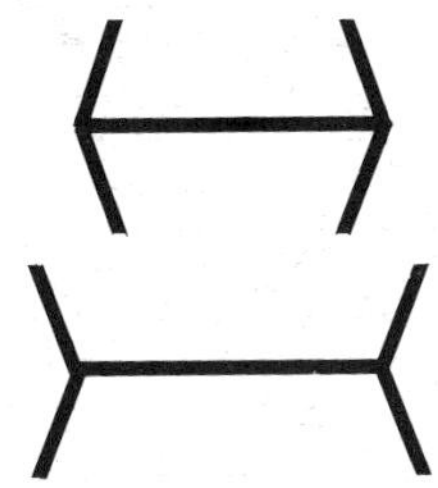

3 Also, our eyes trick us by *not allowing us to see things which are there*. Try closing your left eye and stare with your right eye at the dot in the photograph below. Then, starting at a distance of about 30 cm, move the book slowly toward you. When you reach a certain distance the head of the girl to the right of the dot will disappear.

4 Draw your own illusion.

5 When we say 'I see' we are not always talking about seeing with our eyes. For example, when a teacher explains to us how to solve a particular problem we will often say 'Yes, now I can *see* how it's done', or 'No, I still can't *see* what to do'. When we use 'see' in this way we are talking about **understanding**. Give five other examples of sentences where the word '*see*' is used to mean 'understanding'.

6 The teachings of Jesus say that when we look at ourselves we don't '*see*' or '*understand*' ourselves in the right sort of way. Read John 3:19–20 and explain why (according to Jesus) we don't *see* (understand) ourselves as we should?

7 Explain why Jesus is called 'the light of the world'.

Seeing me

Questions

1 If your house caught fire and you only had time to bring five things out what would they be?

2 Now try to explain why you made this choice.

3 Answer the question of the man in the picture above.

SEEING YOURSELF AS GOD'S GIFT TO THE UNIVERSE

Between the fourteenth and sixteenth centuries many people believed that the Universe was like a small heavenly garden made and looked after by God. It contained 1022 stars all of which remained in the sky because they were fixed to spheres made from crystals. These spheres were thought to revolve around the Earth which stood like God's prize flower at the centre of His garden.

This of course made it easy for people to 'see' themselves as **valuable**. When you are the centre of God's attention you can't really be anything else.

This is perhaps one reason why portraits of people between the fourteenth and sixteenth centuries often look like this.

Henry VIII (King: 1509–47)

Edward VI (King: 1547–53)

Mary I (Queen: 1553–58)

Elizabeth I (Queen: 1558–1603)

Questions and tasks

1 Which of the following words best describe the faces on this page? (You may need a dictionary.)

(You may add words to this list.)

arrogant	self-centred	inferior	questioning	terrified
proud	humble	depressed	inward looking	bitter
meek	frightened	nervous	lost	kind
anxious	superior	self-assured	panicky	jealous

2 a) Why, according to this chapter, do portraits painted between the fourteenth and sixteenth centuries often look as they do?

b) Can you think of any other reasons? The pictures give some clues (e.g. clothes).

3 Read this poem and explain why Warty Bliggens would have felt at home during these centuries.

Warty Bliggens the toad

I met a toad
the other day
by the name
of Warty Bliggens.
He was sitting under
a toadstool
feeling contented.
He explained that when the cosmos
was created
that toadstool was especially
planned for his personal
shelter from sun and rain;
thought out and prepared for him.

Do not tell me
said Warty Bliggens
that there is not a purpose
in the Universe,
the thought is blasphemy.
A little more
conversation revealed
that Warty Bliggens
considers himself to be
the centre of the said Universe.

The earth exists
to grow toadstools for him
to sit under.
The sun to give him light
by day and the moon
and wheeling constellations
to make beautiful the night
for the sake of Warty Bliggens.

4 Most of us at some time in our lives have acted as if we were the centre of the Universe i.e. acting as if other people (like mums, dads and friends) were around only to please us. Draw a picture to illustrate this idea.

SEEING YOURSELF AS NOTHING

Today we know that the Universe is big – really big. So big, in fact, that it contains one hundred billion **galaxies** (cities of stars), with each galaxy containing thousands of millions of stars. Earth is nowhere near the centre. It is a tiny dot in one of these galaxies.

That is why many people today find it difficult to 'see' themselves as *valuable*. 'How can we be valuable,' they say, 'when the Universe is so big and we are so small?'

This is perhaps one reason why twentieth-century portraits often look like this.

Questions and research

1 Which of the words on page 14 best describe the faces on this page?

2 Why, according to this chapter, do twentieth-century portraits often look like this?

3 a) Find a full-faced photograph of yourself when you were at primary school. Write down words which best describe your face then. (You can use words from the list on page 14.)

b) Now find a picture of yourself at secondary school and do the same.

c) If there is a difference between the words you have used for each picture try to explain why you think your face has changed.

d) Some people have said that there is often a difference because primary school children live in the **Universe of Ptolemy** and secondary school children live in the **Universe of Copernicus**. Explain what you think this means. (You will need to find out from the library what Ptolemy and Copernicus said about the Universe.)

AM I VALUABLE?

The reason is simple. Things are not valuable because they are big but because there is somebody around who *values* them. The diamond is valuable because we 'value' it.

THE TEACHINGS OF JESUS

The teachings of Jesus tell us to 'see' ourselves as **valuable** (even though we are small dots in the Universe).

We are all valuable, said Jesus, because there is a God in the Universe who values and cares for us. It is 'His' value and care which makes us valuable.

Jesus expressed this idea with these words:

'For only a penny you can buy two sparrows, yet not one sparrow falls to the ground without your father's consent. As for you, even the hairs of your head have all been counted. So do not be afraid; you are worth much more than many sparrows.'

(Matthew 10:29–31)

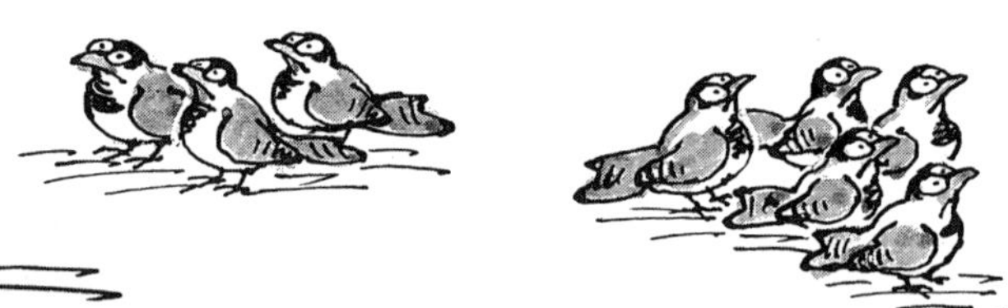

Questions and research

1 What, according to this chapter, makes anything valuable? Do you agree?

2 Which of the following do you 'value' most in others?

good talker	sense of humour
good looks	popular
trusting	clothes
money	kindness
intelligent	

(You may of course add to this list.)

a) Try to put them in order of value.

b) Then try to give reasons for your order.

3 a) Have there been occasions when you have felt that nobody values or cares about you? Give examples.

b) Draw a picture or write a poem to show the feelings and thoughts that go on inside you on these occasions.

4 What, according to Jesus, makes all human beings valuable? (See page 19.)

5 At the time of Jesus children were often treated as if they didn't matter. Read Matthew 18:10–14 and Mark 10:13–16 and explain what Jesus thought.

Seeing God

Questions and tasks

1 When you think of God what idea comes into your mind?

2 Try to explain where you think this idea comes from.

3 Draw a picture of this idea.

A MACHINE-MAKER

Well, I 'see' God as a machine-maker who gave up caring for his machine once he had finished making it.

In other words, God took great care when He made the Universe but then simply flicked the switch to get it working and left it alone to wear itself out. There is no point therefore in praying to God when things go wrong. God never interferes. His job is finished. He expects us to take care of ourselves and do our own repairs. If we can't – tough.

Questions

1 Is there any evidence that God (if He exists) is like a machine-maker who gave up caring for His machine (the world) once it was made?

2 Is there any evidence that God does care about the world and us?

3 Do you think there is any point in praying to God for help when things go wrong?

4 Did Jesus encourage people to ask God for help? (Read Luke 11:1–13.)

A HANGING JUDGE

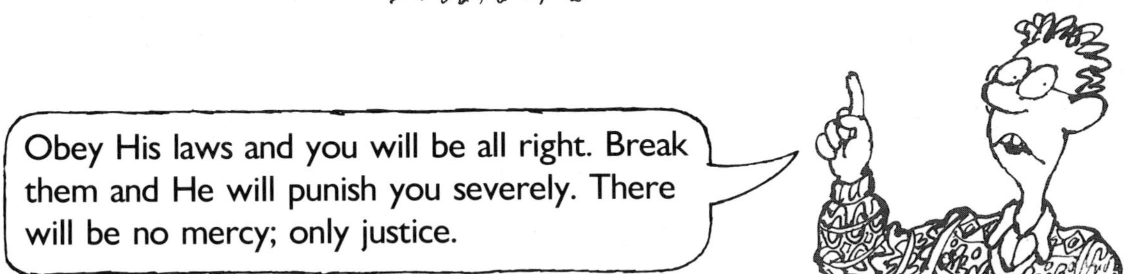

Questions

1 When somebody does something wrong to you, are you the sort who looks for revenge or are you the forgiving type? Give reasons for your answer.

2 Ask five people what type they think you are. Ask them to give their reasons.

3 What type was Jesus? (Read Luke 23:32–4.)

4 If God exists, what type do you think He is?

5 When Jesus said we must forgive each other 70 × 7, what do you think he was trying to say? (Read Matthew 18:21–35.)

6 According to Jesus, what type is God? Read Luke 6:36–8 and explain.

A MAFIA GODFATHER

Questions and research

1 When you join protection rackets, the deal is that you pay money in return for favours – like, protection. Have you ever tried to make a deal with God? Give reasons for your answer and if possible explain what the 'deal' was and what happened.

2 God didn't protect Jesus and stop people crucifying him. Jesus, however, didn't feel cheated. Read Luke 22:39–44 and try to explain why not.

3 At the time of Jesus there were people called Pharisees who spent a lot of their time praying and reading God's Holy Book. Some of these Pharisees thought that by doing this they had become God's favourites. Read Matthew 23:5–7 and 23–8 and explain what Jesus thought about them.

4 What sort of people did Jesus care for? (Read Matthew 9:10–13.)

THE TEACHINGS OF JESUS

When Jesus taught people to pray he told them to call God 'Abba'. This was an Aramaic word (the language Jesus spoke) and it was used by children and grown-ups to address their father. It means 'Dad' or 'Daddy'.

Jesus then taught people to 'see' God as caring for us like a dad – a dad who loves us, who wants us to love Him and who cannot bear to be separated from us.

Jesus told this story to show why God is so much like a dad:

Jesus went on to say, 'There was once a man who had two sons. The younger one said to him, "Father, give me my share of the property now." So the man divided his property between his two sons. After a few days the younger son sold his part of the property and left home with the money. He went to a country far away, where he wasted his money in reckless living. He spent everything he had. Then a severe famine spread over that country, and he was left without a thing. So he went to work for one of the citizens of that country, who sent him out to his farm to take care of the pigs. He wished he could fill himself with the bean pods the pigs ate, but no one gave him anything to eat. At last he came to his senses and said, "All my father's hired workers have more than they can eat, and here I am about to starve! I will get up and go to my father and say, Father, I have sinned against God and against you. I am no longer fit to be called your son; treat me as one of your hired workers." So he got up and started back to his father.

'He was still a long way from home when his father saw him; his heart was filled with pity, and he ran, threw his arms round his son, and kissed him. "Father," the son said, "I have sinned against God and against you. I am no longer fit to be called your son." But the father called his servants. "Hurry!" he said. "Bring the best robe and put it on him. Put a ring on his finger and shoes on his feet. Then go and get the prize calf and kill it, and let us celebrate with a feast! For this son of mine was dead, but now he is alive; he was lost, but now he has been found." And so the feasting began.'

(Luke 15:11–24)

Jesus believed that God is just like the father in this story.

He also cares enough about us to let us leave Him. He doesn't force us to stay. He gives us the freedom to go our own way and if we do He doesn't disown us.

Instead, like an anxious father, He waits for our return and when we come home He rushes out to welcome us. He sees us first and runs to meet us.

There is also no talk of punishment. He is overjoyed that we have returned and accepts us back without lectures, trial periods or new tight rules. His welcome is without conditions.

Jesus therefore invited people to be familiar with God. To come to Him without fear, to call Him father or dad, to enjoy His care, to talk to Him, to listen to Him and to trust Him.

'This is why I tell you not to be worried about the food and drink you need in order to stay alive, or about clothes for your body. After all, isn't life worth more than food? And isn't the body worth more than clothes? Look at the birds: they do not sow seeds, gather a harvest and put it in barns; yet your father in heaven takes care of them! Aren't you worth much more than birds? Can any of you live a bit longer by worrying about it?

'And why worry about clothes? Look how the wild flowers grow: they do not work or make clothes for themselves. But I tell you that not even King Solomon with all his wealth had clothes as beautiful as one of these flowers. It is God who clothes the wild grass – grass that is here today and gone tomorrow, burnt up in the oven. Won't he be all the more sure to clothe you? How little faith you have!

'So do not start worrying: "Where will my food come from? or my drink? or my clothes?" (These are the things the pagans are always concerned about.) Your Father in heaven knows that you need all these things. Instead, be concerned above everything else with the Kingdom of God and with what he requires of you, and he will provide you with all these other things. So do not worry about tomorrow; it will have enough worries of its own. There is no need to add to the troubles each day brings.'

(Matthew 6:25–34)

Questions and research

Do you worry?

1 Which of the following do you worry about? Write them in order of 'worry'. (You may add your own worries to the list.)

- school
- your looks
- money
- what others think of you
- clothes
- family
- baldness
- the future
- spots
- finding a boyfriend or girlfriend

2 Jesus didn't tell people to stop *thinking* about problems. Instead, he told them to stop *worrying*.

a) What are his reasons for saying this?
b) Do you agree with what he says?

3 Jesus called God 'Abba'.

a) What does this mean?
b) Is its 'meaning' a reason why you should stop worrying?

4 In the story on page 26 Jesus tries to show why God is so much like a dad. Explain this in your own words.

5 If Jesus had thought that God was either like a **machine-maker**, a **hanging judge** or a **Mafia Godfather**, how do you think he would have told this story? Choose one of the three types – machine-maker, hanging judge or Mafia Godfather – and rewrite the story.

Seeing belief in God

Question

Do you think that believing in God has got anything to do with the way we behave? Give reasons for your answer.

THE TIGHT-ROPE WALKER

This man is called Blondin. He lived in the nineteenth century and earned his living by walking across tight-ropes. One of his most dangerous walks was across Niagara Falls.

Large crowds would come to watch. On one occasion, Blondin turned to the large crowd and asked: 'Do you believe I can walk across this rope with somebody on my back?'

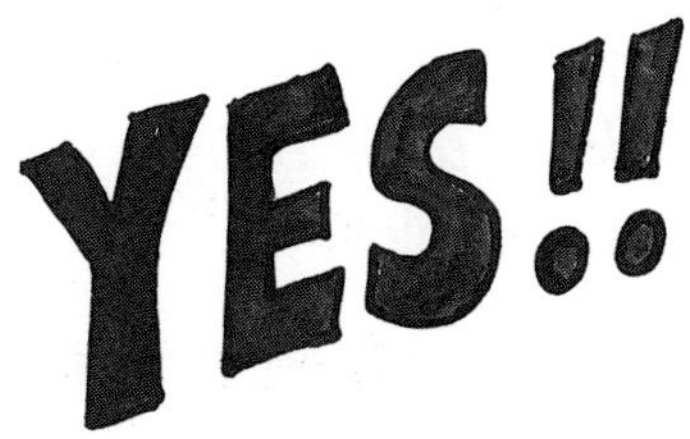

The crowd replied with a loud and enthusiatic: 'YES!'

'Well, if that's the case,' said Blondin, 'one of you get on my back and I'll take you across.'

They all refused.

Questions

1 Who was Blondin?

2 What was the first question Blondin asked the crowd? What did they reply?

3 What did Blondin then challenge the spectators to do? What was their reply?

4 Many would say that the spectators didn't believe Blondin could do it because they wouldn't *back up their beliefs with action*. What do you think?

5 Look at this photograph and explain what you think the person being lifted is believing.

6 Do you have any beliefs that you *back up with action*? Give examples.

THE TEACHINGS OF JESUS

Jesus said that it is not enough to say 'I believe that God exists and is my Father.' Instead, said Jesus, you must be trying to *back up your belief with action* by doing what God wants you to do. This means obeying these commandments:

- 'Love the Lord your God with all your heart, with all your soul, and with all your mind.'
- 'Love your neighbour as you love yourself.'

(Matthew 22:37–9)

To love the Lord your God

There are those who will tell you that if you want to love God then what you have to do is to worship Him every week, read His Holy Book every day and say your prayers regularly.

Jesus said, however, that doing these sort of things wasn't enough. He explained why in the following story.

Don't be a goat

'When the Son of Man comes as King and all the angels with him, he will sit on his royal throne, and the people of all the nations will be gathered before him. Then he will divide them into two groups, just as a shepherd separates the sheep from the goats. He will put the righteous people on his right and the others on his left. Then the King will say to the people on his right, "Come, you that are blessed by my Father! Come and possess the kingdom which has been prepared for you ever since the creation of the world. I was hungry and you fed me, thirsty and you gave me a drink; I was a stranger and you received me in your homes, naked and you clothed me; I was sick and you took care of me, in prison and you visited me."

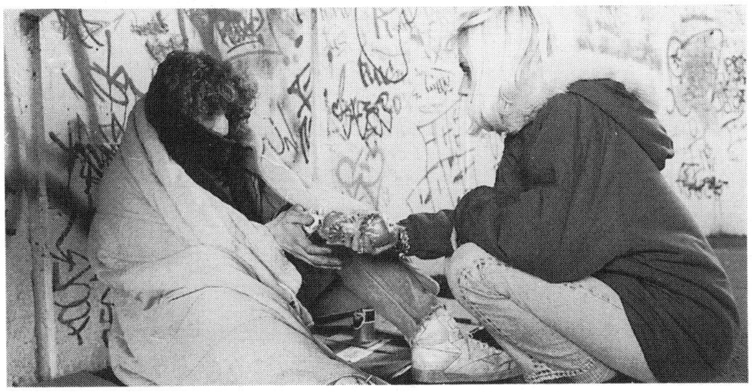

'The righteous will then answer him, "When, Lord, did we ever see you hungry and feed you, or thirsty and give you a drink? When did we ever see you a stranger and welcome you in our homes, or naked and clothe you? When did we ever see you sick or in prison, and visit you?" The King will reply, "I tell you, whenever you did this for one of the least important of these brothers of mine, you did it for me!"

'Then he will say to those on his left, "Away from me, you that are under God's curse! Away to the eternal fire which has been prepared for the Devil and his angels! I was hungry but you would not feed me, thirsty but you would not give me a drink; I was a stranger but you would not welcome me in your homes, naked but you would not clothe me; I was sick and in prison but you would not take care of me."

'Then they will answer him, "When Lord, did we ever see you hungry or thirsty or a stranger or naked or sick or in prison, and would not help you?" The King will reply, "I tell you, whenever you refused to help one of these least important ones, you refused to help me." These, then, will be sent off to eternal punishment, but the righteous will go to eternal life.'

(Matthew 25:31–46)

What Jesus seems to be saying in this story is that no matter what you are doing for God you cannot love him without, at the same time, SEEING OTHER PEOPLE and *loving them.*

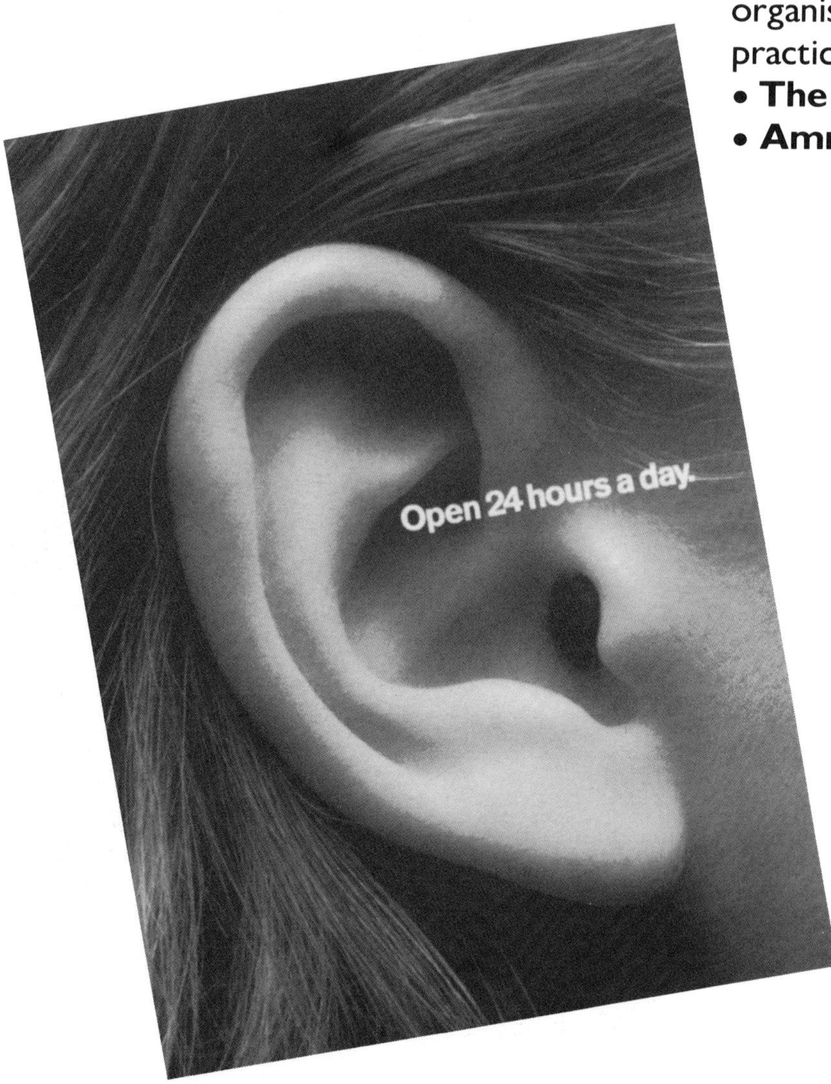

Questions and research

1 Jesus said that if you believe in God then you must back up your belief by obeying two commandments. What are they?

2 In the story of the goats and sheep Jesus shows that the two commandments are connected. Try to explain what this connection is.

3 If you loved others as much as you loved yourself, would your present lifestyle have to change? Give reasons for your answer. (Read 1 Corinthians 13:4–8 before answering the question.)

4 Try to find out how the following organisations put the *teachings* of Jesus into practice:
- **The Samaritans**
- **Amnesty International.**

Seeing you

Question

When new people come to your class do you 'see' them as:

i) intruders?
ii) possible enemies?
iii) possible friends?

(You may add to this list.) Give reasons for your answer.

OTHERS AS INVISIBLE

It is possible to go through life not seeing other people at all.

We can be so much in love with ourselves that we only 'see' ourselves. Other people fade into the background and become *invisible.*

Questions and research

1 When you come to school in the morning what sort of people don't you notice? (*no names, just types*)

2 Have you ever felt that you were invisible to other people? Give examples.

3 Jesus was the type who went out of his way to notice people who were invisible to others. Read the following passages and explain what happened in each case: Matthew 20:29–34; Luke 7:36–50; Luke 19:1–9; Luke 23:32–43.

SEEING OTHERS AS THINGS

We can also go through life looking at people but not actually seeing them as people. Instead we see them as 'things' that we can use and control for our own use.

Questions and research

1 Have you ever treated others as 'things'? Give reasons for your answer.

2 Have others ever treated you as a 'thing'? Give examples.

3 In John 8:1–11 a group of people used a woman as a 'thing' in order to win an argument with Jesus. Explain:

a) what the argument was about;
b) what they wanted to do with the woman;
c) how Jesus treated the woman.

SEEING OTHERS AS SMALLER

There are also times when we may see other people as smaller than ourselves. In other words, we can (for all sorts of reasons) spend our time **looking down** on others. It may, for example, be because. . .

. . .they don't look like us;

. . .they don't sound like us;

. . .they don't dress like us;

. . .or they don't act like us.

But whatever the reason, on these occasions we see others as less important and less valuable than ourselves.

Questions and research

1 Have you ever been in a place where you have felt that people were 'looking down' at you? Try to give examples.

2 Draw a picture or write a poem to illustrate how you felt on these occasions.

3 What sort of people do you tend to look down on? (*no names, just types*) Explain why.

4 At the time of Jesus many people *looked down* on tax collectors because they worked for the Romans. Read Luke 19:1–9 and explain how Jesus treated these people.

SEEING OTHERS AS BIGGER

There may also be times when we see others as bigger than ourselves. In other words, for all sorts of reasons we can spend our time **looking up** to others.

For example, they may be famous.

They may be extremely good looking.

They may have pots of money and style...

...or simply have more power.

But whatever the reason, we can turn these people into gods and hero-worship them. We begin then to see these people as being more important and more valuable than ourselves.

Questions and research

1 List the names of people who are hero-worshipped today.

2 What sort of people make you feel small and unimportant?

3 Try to explain why.

4 Who did Jesus say were the greatest? (Read Mark 9:33–7.)

THE TEACHINGS OF JESUS

Jesus reminded people that we all share the same Heavenly Father.

He taught people to see each other as BROTHERS AND SISTERS.

Therefore nobody, said Jesus, should be invisible; nobody should be treated as a 'thing'; and nobody should be looked down upon or looked up to as a god.

Instead we should love one another as family.

Questions and research

1 If you began to see all other people as members of your family would this change the way you behave? Give reasons for your answer.

2 Jesus believed that it should change our behaviour. Read Matthew 5:43–8 and explain how Jesus thought we should change.

HOW DO I LOVE OTHERS?

Jesus didn't answer this question by giving long lists of instructions telling us in the smallest detail how we should love each other. He understood that instructions, no matter how many were given, would never be able to cover all the different sorts of ways we might have to love.

Instead Jesus answered this question by giving us a number of **signposts** – signposts which simply point our love in the right sort of direction. It will become clearer what this means if we now look at some of these **signposts**.

Imagine somebody in your school being 'invisible'; in other words, the sort of person who is never noticed by others. Every day at school they are ignored, isolated and only spoken to when somebody is picking on them or making a joke at their expense.

WHAT SHOULD YOU DO IN THIS SITUATION?

Well, the teachings of Jesus don't try to tell you 'exactly' what you should be doing. What they do say, however, is that if you are to 'love God and love others' then the 'invisible' people in your school should become 'visible'; for whatever you decide to do should be guided by a desire to be on the side of the weak, the neglected and the oppressed.

Questions and research

1 What do you think you would do in this situation? Give reasons for your answer.

2 Read Matthew 9:9–13 and explain why Jesus spent so much time with those rejected by others.

Imagine somebody coming up to you during breaktime and accusing you falsely of spreading lies about them. While they are having a go at you, they get more and more worked up and eventually end up treating you like a 'thing' and smacking you in the mouth. In that situation many people would feel that they had a 'right' to smack the person back and would probably end up doing so, especially if the other person was small and weak-looking.

WHAT SHOULD YOU DO IN THIS SITUATION?

Once again, the teachings of Jesus don't try to tell you 'exactly' what you should do. What they do say, however, is that if you are to 'love God and love others' then whatever you decide to do should not always be guided by what you feel you have a 'right' to do. Sometimes, said Jesus, we must actually give up our 'rights' and be guided instead by a desire **to make peace**.

Questions and research

1 What do you think you would do in this situation?

2 Some people say that violence creates more problems than it solves. What do you think this means? Do you agree?

3 School pupils sometimes go on about their '*rights*' especially when they are being told off by a teacher. Make a list of the sorts of 'rights' they often claim to have.

4 Jesus said that people's behaviour should be guided by LOVE and not always by *'rights'*.

a) Read Matthew 5:38–42 and explain the sort of 'rights' Jesus said we must *sometimes* be prepared to give up. (Remember he wasn't issuing commands that *always* had to be obeyed.)

b) Illustrate your answers with pictures.

Finally, imagine you are the sort of person who others of your own age **look up to**. They tend to copy you, do what you say and follow you around. You find yourself therefore in a position of power where you could if you wished 'look down' on these people and control them.

WHAT SHOULD YOU DO IN THIS SITUATION?
Well, once again there are no precise instructions. The teachings of Jesus do say, however, that if you are to 'love God and love others' then your actions should be guided by a desire to **serve** others rather than turn others into slaves and **be served**.

Questions and research

1 Have you ever been surrounded by people that you could have controlled and used for your own benefit? Give examples and explain what happened.

2 a) When Jesus was in this situation what did he do? (Read John 13:3–15.)
b) What do you think Jesus was trying to teach by doing this?

3 In this book we have been looking at those teachings of Jesus which tell us that if we want to be happy then we must begin to **see ourselves, God, belief and each other in a new light**.
a) In your own words, summarise these teachings.
b) Do you think that you could be happier if you began to 'see' these things differently? Give reasons for your answer.